... although not comparable to
Scotland!

Thank you, Russell and Margaret
for helping us plan our
wonderful trip!

Robbie, Dominique,
Brigitte, Hardy

(MAY 2018)

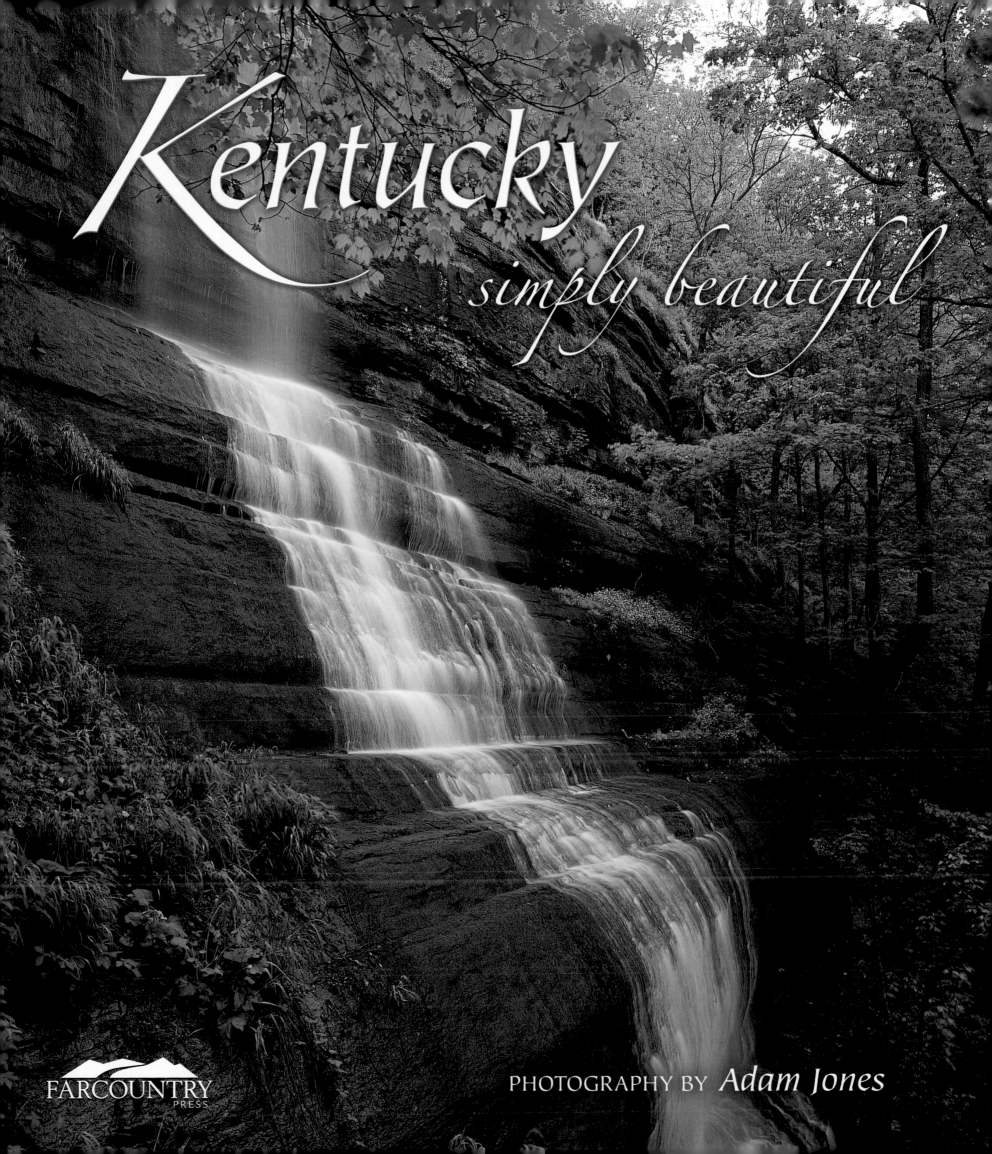

Kentucky
simply beautiful

FARCOUNTRY PRESS

PHOTOGRAPHY BY *Adam Jones*

TITLE PAGE: A waterfall glides down the Kentucky River Palisades.

RIGHT: At Louisville, a phalanx of ancient trees stands guard.

FRONT COVER: Wind, water, and ice eroded the soft sandstone, creating the 50- by 90-foot Natural Arch in Daniel Boone National Forest.

BACK COVER: Nature's palette brightens an overcast day near Louisville.

FRONT FLAP: A field of sunflowers near the capital city of Frankfort turns toward the sun.

ISBN 10: 1-56037-395-4
ISBN 13: 978-1-56037-395-7
Photography © 2006 by Adam Jones
© 2006 Farcountry Press
Text by Adam Jones

For more information about our books write Farcountry Press, P.O. Box 5630, Helena, MT 59604; call (800) 821-3874; or visit www.farcountrypress.com.

Created, produced, and designed in the United States. Printed in China.

11 10 09 08 07 06   1 2 3 4 5

INTRODUCTION *by Adam Jones*

As a young boy growing up in Kentucky's Jefferson County, I awoke each morning anticipating the joy of discovery each day promised. Every summer, my childhood friends and I spent countless hours exploring the creeks, ponds, and woodlots around my hometown of Louisville in search of wondrous treasures and interesting creatures. I fancied myself a modern-day explorer, like Daniel Boone, discovering different types of fish, crawfish, snakes, birds, and small mammals. Camping with my parents and younger brother in Kentucky's state parks was the highlight of the summer. At the time, I had no idea that those experiences in Kentucky's open spaces would later impact my life in a big way.

Fast forward a couple of decades: I wed my high school sweetheart, Sherrie, to whom I'm still happily married. I borrowed a 35mm camera to snap a few shots of our Hawaiian honeymoon and returned home completely hooked on photography. Unleashing my newfound passion, I now had the perfect excuse to return to that childlike exploration of the world—only this time I would do it through the lens of a camera. I photographed everything around me—birds, bugs, reptiles, amphibians, landscapes—even venturing underwater!

Although my career as a nature and travel photographer has taken me to some of the world's most exotic locations, Kentucky is home. Photographing the place I call home affords me the time to look closer and dig deeper into what is meaningful. Sitting at my computer writing the introduction to this book, I glance through my office window at the stately dogwood and redbud trees in magnificent bloom. Cardinals are singing from the branches, and bees are buzzing around the purple redbud flowers. Warm, gentle breezes carry the smell of spring flowers, bluegrass, and fragrant trees and shrubs. Ah, spring in Kentucky—there simply is no better place.

The Bluegrass State remains a great place to live, a place where neighbors still care about one another and take the time to chat across the back yard fence. Even the two largest cites—Louisville and Lexington—still offer a friendly home-town atmosphere. Louisville may be the sixteenth-largest city in the United States, but it hasn't lost its small-town charm.

Not only is Kentucky blessed with an abundance of gentle mountains, hills, forests, prairies, streams, lakes, meandering rivers, wildflowers, and wildlife, it has a rich cultural heritage. The Shawnee Indians used the area now known as Kentucky as a hunting ground. Settlers from Virginia and North Carolina arrived in the late 1770s, and Kentucky became the fifteenth state in 1792, the same year that Frankfort was named the capital city.

Louisville is home of the world-famous Churchill Downs and the Kentucky Derby, first leg of horseracing's Triple Crown. Some of the most famous and picturesque horse farms in the world are found in the Bluegrass Region, with Lexington at its center.

Kentucky's Bluegrass Region is also know for its Southern hospitality and historical attractions, including the state's famous bourbon industry, where distillers such as Woodford Reserve, Maker's Mark, Wild Turkey, and Buffalo Trace practice the art of bourbon making—95 percent of the bourbon whiskey produced in the U.S. comes from Kentucky.

The photographs in this book were not made with the ultimate goal of creating a book; instead they are images of what I enjoy and treasure most about this beautiful state.

LEFT: Bad Branch State Nature Preserve protects 2,343 acres of lush Bad Branch Gorge near Whitesburg.

RIGHT: Many of America's earliest maintained roads were privately owned, and tolls covered the cost of care. Dillon Asher (1774 to 1844), the first tollgate keeper on Kentucky's Wilderness Road, built this cabin in the late 1700s.

ABOVE: Hadley Pottery in Louisville hand-produces dinnerware and decorative stoneware. M. A. (Mary Alice) Hadley, a painter who turned to pottery design in 1940, created all of the designs.

LEFT: Quaint and friendly describe the community of Washington, where this welcome was found. The 1700s village of log cabins, museums, antiques and craft shops, and taverns is now part of Maysville.

FACING PAGE: Inside the monument at Abraham Lincoln Birthplace National Historic Site stands a replica one-room log cabin, similar to the one in which the future president was born on February 12, 1809. Congress set aside land for the memorial in 1916, which occupies about one third of Thomas and Nancy Lincoln's 348.5-acre farm.

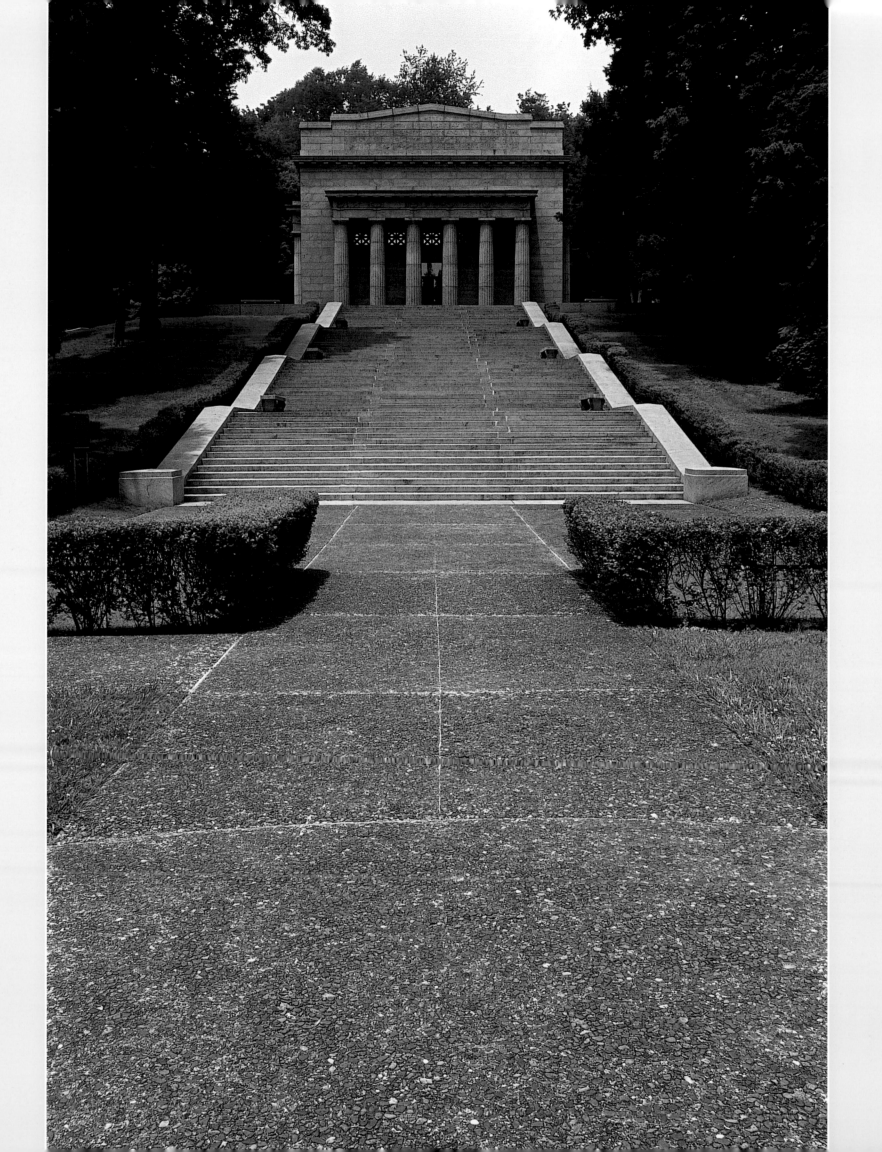

BOTH PAGES: Re-enactors annually commemorate the Battle of Perryville, which took place on October 8, 1862. Confederate and Union forces—both racing toward Louisville—met in a battle that cost 1,355 lives and left 5,486 men wounded, with 766 listed as captured or missing. Union forces prevented the Confederacy from capturing Louisville and taking the state of Kentucky.

ABOVE: Street rodders bring their restored and customized pre-1949 automobiles to Louisville's Kentucky Exposition Center for the Street Rod Nationals.

LEFT: For eleven days in late August, the Kentucky State Fair in Louisville features carnival rides, champion livestock shows, cooking and flower-arranging competitions, talent contests, and plenty of food and music.

LEFT: A white-breasted nuthatch pauses in its usual head-first creep down a tree trunk.

RIGHT: Sarah Bush Johnston, future step-mother of Abraham Lincoln, was born at Elizabethtown—where this memorial to her stands—in 1788. She and Thomas Lincoln, who had known each other in their youth, had both lost their spouses when they met again. They married in Elizabethtown, and their blended family of two Lincoln children and a Lincoln cousin, plus three Johnston children, farmed in Indiana and Illinois.

BELOW: Visitors to Fort Boonesborough can watch resident artisans at work and learn what life was like here for founder Daniel Boone and other residents. The settlement, initiated on April 1, 1775, near modern Richmond, was Kentucky's second after Fort Harrod at Harrodsburg.

ABOVE: Nearing day's end, a Lake Cumberland water-skier creates a golden wake. The 101-mile-long lake was created by the Wolf Creek Dam, built on the Cumberland River in 1950.

FACING PAGE: Sailboats are one way to enjoy 184-mile-long Kentucky Lake on the Tennessee River. These are resting at Lighthouse Landing Resort and Marina in Grand Rivers.

LEFT: Coal mined in Kentucky is shipped around the globe and is used to produce 17 percent of the world's electricity.

FAR LEFT: After crossing the Cumberland Gap, from 200,000 to 300,000 people—between 1775 and 1810—moved along this road near Middlesboro for better lives on the western frontier.

BELOW: A barge loaded with coal pushes up the Ohio River past Otter Creek and toward Louisville.

LEFT: An American saddlebred horse peers out from a barn in Lexington's Kentucky Horse Park.

FACING PAGE: Churchill Downs at Louisville may be most famous for that single race in May, the Kentucky Derby, but the track also hosts thoroughbred racing in the spring and fall.

BELOW: Thoroughbreds also race at Keeneland, west of Lexington in the famed Bluegrass Region. The track ranks among the top-ten horseracing facilities in the United States.

ABOVE: Kayaking is a popular weekend getaway, and this boater is enjoying a paddle on Elkhorn Creek near Frankfort.

RIGHT: Lake Cumberland reflects the summer sky near Somerset. Besides delighting recreationists, the south-central Kentucky lake generates power and helps control floods.

ABOVE: Housed in a historic grocery store in Morehead and managed by Morehead State University, the Kentucky Folk Art Center houses approximately 1,000 pieces of Appalachian folk art.

RIGHT: The Covington–Cincinnati Bridge was completed in 1866 to link Covington to Cincinnati, Ohio. It was the world's first suspension bridge with both vertical suspenders and diagonal stays fanning from its towers. In 1984, the bridge was renamed the John A. Roebling Suspension Bridge in honor of its builder, who used the same principles for his design of the Brooklyn Bridge two decades later.

RIGHT: The sun drops below the horizon at Long Run Park in Jefferson County.

BELOW: Mammoth Cave National Park was established in 1941 to preserve the cave system, including Mammoth Cave, the scenic river valleys of the Green and Nolin rivers, and a portion of south-central Kentucky. It is the longest recorded cave system in the world, with more than 360 miles explored and mapped.

24

The Dix River flows two miles from the dam of the same name before emptying into the Kentucky River.

ABOVE: Sunflowers bloom near Union in northern Kentucky. Both the stiff and the woodland varieties are native, but the state flower is the goldenrod.

LEFT: A two-day-old Arabian foal and its mother take their exercise in a field of buttercups near Louisville.

ABOVE (TOP): Every corvette starts life at Bowling Green, which is fittingly the home of the National Corvette Museum. Pictured is the interior of the museum's trademark Sky Dome.

ABOVE (BOTTOM): Fast and dangerous, hydroplane racing takes place on the Ohio River near Milton.

RIGHT: The AAA affiliate of the Cincinnati Reds since 2000, the Louisville Bats play in Louisville Slugger Field. Their home park is named for the locally made premier baseball bat, but their logo features the flying mammal.

ABOVE: Ashland's Central Park, a horseracing track until 1923, provides forty-seven acres of recreational facilities for children and adults. Its lily pond features three floating fountains.

RIGHT: Cumberland Falls State Resort Park features campgrounds, cabins, and deluxe rooms—all with trail access to features like the striking Dog Slaughter Falls.

ABOVE: A park ranger stops at the Frozen Niagara formation in Mammoth Cave National Park, which is both a United Nations World Heritage Site and an International Biosphere Reserve.

RIGHT: Tobacco cures in an open-sided tobacco barn in central Kentucky.

ABOVE (TOP): A male northern cardinal poses for the camera amid crabapple blossoms. Kentuckians chose the cardinal as their state bird.

ABOVE (BOTTOM): This hand pump once was the answer to a family's prayers: Life would be easier now that they could fill the water pails right outside the back door.

LEFT: Hybrid poppies grace a classic Springfield-area farm.

FACING PAGE: The rising sun silhouettes trees on a winter day in northwestern Kentucky. Temperatures here at this time of year are generally mild, ranging from 27°F to 43°F—with a few days of snow during January and February.

BELOW: A spiral staircase winds through the Trustees' Office building in the Shaker Village of Pleasant Hill, near Harrodsburg. Costumed interpreters in fourteen restored buildings describe the nineteenth-century religious sect's principles of simple living, celibacy, and worship through song and dance. Artisans demonstrate crafts of the era.

LEFT: Trail of Tears Commemorative Park in Hopkinsville preserves one of the few documented campsites along the path by which Cherokee people moved from their mountain homeland to Indian Territory (now Oklahoma) in 1838 and 1839. Two chiefs—Fly Smith and Whitepath—who died and were buried here are honored in this sculpture by Steve Shields.

FAR LEFT: Natural Arch, in Daniel Boone National Forest, is fifty feet high and ninety feet long.

BELOW: A white-tailed doe surveys her surroundings in a western Kentucky tall-grass field.

RIGHT: South of Lexington, Jessamine Creek steps its way down toward its mouth on the Kentucky River.

BELOW: An eastern gray squirrel hunts for a wintertime meal.

ABOVE: Open to the public for guided tours, this is the birthplace and childhood home of country singer Loretta Lynn, in Butcher Hollow ("holler," locally) near Van Lear in the Eastern Coal Field.

LEFT: Jenny Wiley State Resort Park is named for the pioneer woman captured, along with family members, by Indians in 1789 and held for eleven months. Before her escape, she witnessed the slayings of her brother and children. In today's park, Queen Anne's lace and spotted touch-me-nots grow on the shore of Dewey Lake.

ABOVE: Handmade items crafted in traditional Shaker style—like these straw brooms—are for sale at the Shaker Village of Pleasant Hill in Harrodsburg.

RIGHT: Wheat, ripe for harvesting, waves near Louisville.

LEFT: Tiny ruby-crowned kinglets, weighing only a quarter of an ounce, live and sing high in conifer trees, where a pair produces an unusually high average of eight eggs annually.

FAR LEFT: Mill Creek Lake in Daniel Boone National Forest mirrors bright autumn colors and soft mountain mist.

BELOW: The mountaintop Pine Mountain State Resort Park, overlooking Kentucky Ridge State Forest, became Kentucky's first state park in 1924. Native stone like this was used in building its Herndon J. Evans Lodge.

LEFT: White Hall State Historic Site was once the home of Cassius Marcellus Clay, an emancipationist and friend of President Lincoln. Costumed guides describe the 1860s-era furnishings and the blend of Georgian-Italianate architecture.

FACING PAGE: This cupola-topped barn at the 275-acre Manchester Farm near Lexington is home to a thoroughbred racehorse breeding program.

BELOW: Horses graze on the bluegrass at Kentucky Horse Park in Lexington.

LEFT: Flowering dogwood blossoms lend their delicate touch to a foggy spring day along the Kentucky River Palisades.

FACING PAGE: Although Red River Gorge Geological Area protects rock arches and natural shelters, on this winter day trees frosted with snow and ice grab the spotlight.

BELOW: The *Mississippi Queen* steamboat, seen docked at Maysville on the Ohio River, carries 422 passengers and the custom-built, world's largest calliope. It has been in passenger service since 1976.

RIGHT: The cecropia moth has a wingspan of up to six inches and is the largest moth in North America.

FAR RIGHT: Come along this trail in Red River Gorge Geological Area to enjoy the crisp smells and the crunch of leaves on an early autumn day.

BELOW: An exhibit inside Owensboro's International Bluegrass Music Museum helps to tell the story of the commercial yet folk-based musical style that combines fast-tempo banjo, fiddle, and bass with jazz-style improvisations.

ABOVE: General Butler State Park near Carrollton—viewed here on a foggy, humid summer day—honors William Orlando Butler, of the family prominent in military matters from before the American Revolution through the Civil War.

FACING PAGE: High Bridge, spanning the Kentucky River's Gorge and Palisades, was North America's first cantilever bridge and the world's highest one over a navigable river. It served railroad trains from 1877 through 1976.

FOLLOWING PAGES: Muhammad Ali was born Cassius Marcellus Clay Jr. in Louisville, Kentucky, on January 17, 1942. The Muhammad Ali Center preserves the legacy and ideals of the boxing champion, seeking to promote respect, hope, and understanding, and to inspire both adults and children to be the best they can be.

ABOVE: An Alexander Calder sculpture, *The Red Feather*, stands in the forecourt of Louisville's Kentucky Center for the Arts, home to innovative performing arts productions.

RIGHT: Three floors of interactive exhibits and live demonstrations bring history to life in the Frazier International History Museum in Louisville.

ABOVE: A faithful old barn and buttercups near Central City simmer in the summer sun.

FACING PAGE: Trees are beginning to leaf out across Cumberland Falls State Park near Corbin.

RIGHT: Eastern cottontails are solitary animals that guard their territories, hide out during the middle of the day, and elude predators by zig-zagging at speeds of up to fifteen miles an hour.

ABOVE: Whitehaven Welcome Center in Paducah was built in the 1860s and then received many additions over the years. Abandoned in 1968, it was heavily damaged by weather and vandals before being moved to its present site and restored beginning in 1981.

FACING PAGE: The free-flowing Big South Fork of the Cumberland River is a haven for non-motorized boating in Big South Fork National River and Recreation Area.

ABOVE: Ashland House in Lexington stands at the site of the original home of American statesman Henry Clay (1777 to 1852), his wife Lucretia, and their four children. Clay named his 600-acre estate "Ash Land" for its extensive groves of ash trees. The current house was built by son James in 1857, and its interior now exhibits 1860s furnishings.

FACING PAGE: The Cathedral Basilica of the Assumption serves Kentucky's Diocese of Covington in the northern and eastern counties. It was built by local craftsmen beginning in 1895, with the exterior largely complete by 1910. The exterior French Gothic architecture includes a façade modeled on that of Notre Dame in Paris, and the interior is modeled on the Abbey Church of St. Denis, also in Paris.

ABOVE: One raindrop on a daisy's petal reflects the image of another flower for the camera.

LEFT: Black-eyed susans and cosmos carpet a field near Union.

ABOVE: Greenbo Lake State Resort Park near Greenup offers conference facilities, a swimming pool with waterslide, hiking, horseback riding, biking, canoeing, and fishing.

LEFT: Bald eagles, symbol of the United States, made a great recovery after eggshell-thinning DDT was banned and the bird was placed on the Endangered Species List. They've been reported in Cumberland, Harlan, and Logan counties— and occasionally along the Ohio River.

FAR LEFT: Where the Russell Fork River carved a five-mile-long, 1,600-foot-deep canyon, Breaks Interstate Park on the Kentucky–Virginia border invites visitors to twelve miles of hiking trails and four scenic overlooks.

ABOVE: Brush Arbor Appalachian Pioneer Log Village at Renfro Valley, south of Lexington, demonstrates pioneer life with ten restored log cabins and a log church that holds Sunday services.

RIGHT: Could it be that this well-dressed angler was just passing by and simply couldn't resist this small eastern Jefferson County lake?

RIGHT: Centre Family Dwelling is the largest of thirty-four original buildings at the Shaker Village of Pleasant Hill. The Shaker faithful lived in large "families" regardless of blood ties, and up to eighty lived in this limestone building of forty rooms, including a meeting room, dining room, and suite of infirmary rooms.

BELOW: The tulips are beginning to open at the Mary Todd Lincoln House in Lexington. The family of the future wife of Abraham Lincoln moved here when she was a teenager, remodeling an inn built around 1803 to 1806.

ABOVE: Hidden River Cave, in the city of Horse Cave, holds a river flowing 150 feet below ground. The water was harnessed to provide electricity in the 1890s, making Horse Cave—in south-central Kentucky's Cave Country—the second commonwealth city to have the new form of energy.

FACING PAGE: Follow this path through the blue-eyed marys to enjoy part of Lexington's 470-acre Raven Run Nature Sanctuary. Ten miles of hiking trails lead to streams, meadows, and woodlands that are home to 600 plant species and host 200 bird species throughout the year.

RIGHT AND BELOW: Alabama-born father of the blues W. C. Handy first tasted success when he joined an Evansville, Indiana, band that toured the region. When they played for a Henderson, Kentucky, barbecue in 1896, Handy met the woman who soon became his wife. Today, Henderson celebrates with a week-long W. C. Handy Blues and Barbecue Festival.

FAR RIGHT: Yes, *do* play in the Dancing Waters fountain to cool off at Louisville's 72-acre Waterfront Park on the Ohio River.

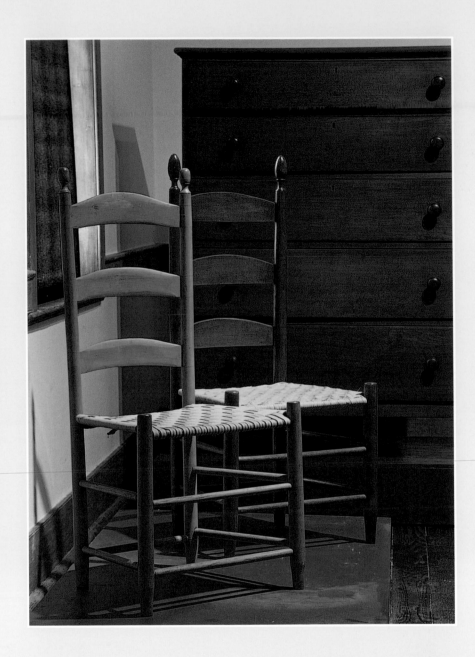

ABOVE: Shakertown at South Union exhibits the plain lines of Shaker handcrafted furniture, and its museum also tells how the communal sect introduced crop rotation to southern Kentucky, packaged garden seeds, raised new strains of livestock, ran a successful inn, and adopted mechanical farm machinery. This community existed from 1807 to 1922.

RIGHT: Might the next Kentucky Derby winner be relaxing among this group of thoroughbreds near Shelbyville?

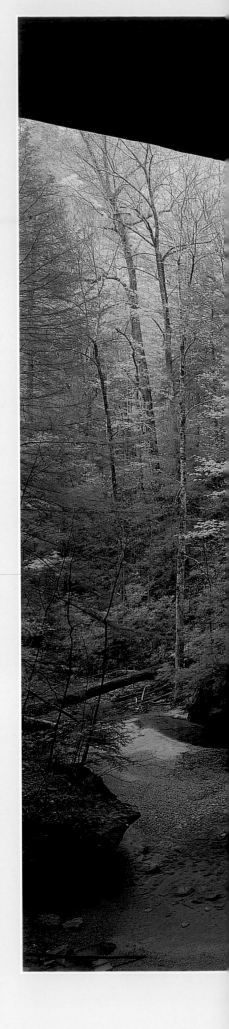

ABOVE: Seventy-eight feet long and sixty-five feet high, the sandstone Natural Bridge is the centerpiece of Natural Bridge State Resort Park near Slade. Visitors can enjoy a chairlift ride up the mountainside to the arch.

RIGHT: At two days old, a white-tailed deer fawn stays still and depends on its camouflage coat for safe hiding.

Near Whitley City, a woodland trail takes visitors to, and then behind, the 113-foot-high Yahoo Falls. Spring is the time to visit, when the water runs its fullest—during summer, it fades to a trickle.

LEFT: Federal Hill mansion in My Old Kentucky Home State Park in Bardstown was home of the Rowan family. While their cousin Stephen Foster was visiting in 1852, some say he wrote one of his most poplar sentimental songs here. Today, costumed guides escort visitors through the mansion and its formal garden.

RIGHT: Morning mist rises on a cool autumn morning in Red River Gorge Geological Area.

BELOW: Octagonal homes were fashionable in the mid–nineteenth century, when they were thought to receive more natural light and be easier to heat and keep cool. Octagon Hall Museum north of Franklin preserves the 1843 home of Andrew Jackson Caldwell, who welcomed Confederate soldiers to camp on the grounds during the Civil War; the generals were invited to rest indoors.

ABOVE: Traditional crafts offer modern careers, as with this basket-weaver.

RIGHT: The Big South Fork of the Cumberland River flows undammed along its boulder-strewn route for ninety miles through Big South Fork National River and Recreation Area. Non-motorized recreation is welcomed on and along the stream.

LEFT: Have dinner and socialize at Covington Landing, while viewing the Cincinnati skyline across the Ohio River.

BELOW: Louisville converted an enclosed downtown mall to the open-air Fourth Street Live!—which became the city's premier entertainment, dining, and retail district.

RIGHT: On College Square in Berea, Boone Tavern has operated since 1909, its hotel and restaurant staffed by Berea College students and furnished with their handmade woodcraft. The top-ranked college requires all students to work at least ten hours per week in addition to carrying full academic schedules.

BELOW: The Appalachian dulcimer, brought to the mountains in the early 1800s by Scots-Irish immigrants, can be plucked, strummed, or bowed to make music, traditionally with one string following the melody and two others producing a background drone. Most dulcimers have three or four strings, like this one made by Warren A. May of Berea.

RIGHT: Refreshing Tioga Falls near Radcliff is reached by a two-mile loop trail through Fort Knox—which may be closed for military training operations as well as during hunting season.

BELOW: Hensley Settlement in the Cumberland Gap National Historical Park near Middlesboro began on Brush Mountain in 1903-1904. The Hensleys and Gibbons moved here to clear the land, build log houses, and farm—without electricity or machinery. Now refurbished, twenty-five buildings—including the Finley Hensley house, pictured here, a schoolhouse, and a blacksmith and carpentry shop—served from fifty to one hundred people.

LEFT: Helm Roberts designed Kentucky's Vietnam Veterans Memorial in Frankfort to honor each lost soldier individually. The giant stainless-steel sundial pointer sits at the center of a round granite plaza engraved with their 1,103 names, which are arranged so that the shadow daily points to the names of soldiers lost on that date.

BELOW: Kingdom Come State Park near Cumberland was named for the popular Civil War–era novel *The Little Shepherd of Kingdom Come* and offers four spectacular wilderness overlooks of Black Mountain and the Cumberland Plateau. This view is looking east toward the sunrise.

RIGHT: The Kentucky Derby, known as "The Most Exciting Two Minutes in Sports," is held annually at Churchill Downs in Louisville on the first Saturday in May. The derby is the first leg of the Triple Crown of Thoroughbred Racing.

BELOW: Red fox pups pose for the camera. Common in Kentucky, foxes eat mostly plants during the summer and primarily consume meat during the winter.

ABOVE: This Jefferson Davis Monument stands in Fairview, the town where the future president of the Confederate States of America was born in 1808.

LEFT: An Appalachian Mountains sunrise is viewed from high atop Pine Mountain Resort Park.

ABOVE: Only one man is buried beneath Maplewood Cemetery's Wooldridge Monuments in Mayfield: Col. Henry Wooldridge, whose Italian-marble image towers above sandstone portraits of his mother, four brothers, three sisters, two nieces, Wooldridge on his horse Fop, two of his hunting dogs, a deer, and a fox. The colonel, a horse breeder and trader who never married, commissioned the statues in the 1890s and was buried here in 1899.

RIGHT: Pennyrile Forest State Resort Park's name reflects the local western Kentucky pronunciation for pennyroyal, the mint-family herb found in these thick woods. Pennyrile Lake, seen here, is open for swimming, canoeing, motorboating, and fishing.

RIGHT: Daniel Boone ended up with two graves, fitting for a man who moved from Pennsylvania to Kentucky and, when its frontier became "crowded," went farther west. For this one, at Frankfort, his bones were transported from the grave beside Rebecca Boone (who preceded him in death) at Defiance, Missouri, where Daniel died in 1820. But some people say he had been buried at Rebecca's feet because the grave beside hers already was filled—no one is certain.

FACING PAGE: Buy some freshly ground cornmeal at McHargue's Mill, a working reproduction on the Little Laurel River in Levi Jackson State Park surrounded by the nation's largest exhibit of millstones. The original McHargue family mills were built in the 1850s.

BELOW: A catalpa tree in bloom sets off Bennett's Mill Bridge, northwest of Ashland. Built in 1855, the 195-foot bridge across Tygarts Creek is one of Kentucky's longest covered bridges—and is now closed to traffic.

ABOVE: Separate stairs and doorways for men and women were part of Shaker living, as seen here in the Centre House of The Shaker Museum at South Union—the westernmost Shaker religious community—built in 1824. Exhibits includes furniture, textiles, wooden tools, and baskets.

RIGHT: Thoroughbred racing champion Cigar, born in 1990 and now living in Kentucky Horse Park's Hall of Champions, won sixteen consecutive races between 1994 and 1996 (matching the record of Citation), had an unbeaten 1995 season, and earned nearly one billion dollars during his career. Among Cigar's ancestors are Seattle Slew and Northern Dancer.

LEFT: Tree-respecting fences mark off pastures at a classic Kentucky Bluegrass horse farm.

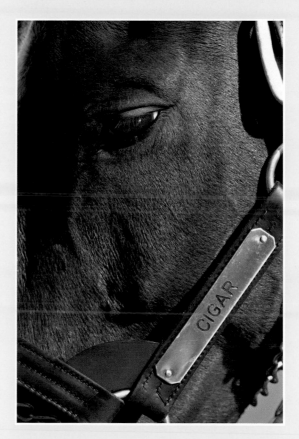

RIGHT: Junior looks out at the world from his birthplace and home, a sycamore tree—one of the raccoon's favorite den trees.

FACING PAGE: A new day begins along the Kentucky River Palisades in Jessamine County.

BELOW: Fifteen thousand years ago, when ice sheets extended to the other side of the Ohio River, giant mastodons, wooly mammoths, and ground sloths gathered around warm salt springs near today's town of Union. Big Bone Lick State Park exhibits some of the fossilized bones in its museum, while this outdoor display shows how the animals became trapped (and preserved) in the area's "jelly" soil.

Stock cars, Indy cars, motorcycles, and trucks race in various events at the 1.5-mile, 14-turn, tri-oval Kentucky Speedway, which opened at Sparta in 2000.

LEFT: Flags of the United States fly above those of the Commonwealth of Kentucky. Along with Massachusetts, Pennsylvania, and Virginia, Kentucky retained the historic term for a state or nation governed by its residents. Legally, no difference from "states" existed after the first three ratified the U.S. Constitution—and Kentucky was admitted to the Union in 1792.

BELOW: At My Old Kentucky Home State Park, visitors enjoy the stage presentation *The Stephen Foster Story.* Foster (1826 to 1864) was the first hugely successful composer of American pop music, writing 200 songs that were sung in music halls and along the pioneer trails, including "My Old Kentucky Home," "O! Susanna!" and "Beautiful Dreamer." Sheet-music publishers made all the money, and Foster died penniless.

ABOVE: Kentucky's "Bourbon Trail" includes tours of six major bourbon distilleries, including Maker's Mark—whose copper stills are seen here—where visitors witness how "America's only native spirit" has been manufactured for 200 years.

RIGHT: Sunset creates a mystical moment over Kentucky Lake's Smith Bay, seen from Land Between the Lakes National Recreation Area. The area is bounded on the west by the Tennessee River's Kentucky Lake, and on the east by the Cumberland River's Lake Barkley.

ABOVE: Kentucky's Beaux Arts–style capitol in Frankfort was dedicated in 1910. It is the commonwealth's fourth state house and was constructed after the General Assembly chose Frankfort (instead of Lexington or Louisville) as the capital city.

FACING PAGE: The Dix River flows between Garrard and Mercer counties.

ABOVE: Since 1972, the tallest building in downtown Louisville's skyline has been the forty-story National City Tower, which belongs to a banking corporation, followed by the domed, thirty-five-story AEGON insurance company building.

FACING PAGE: Thunder over Louisville, one of the nation's largest fireworks displays, is just one of many events leading up to the Kentucky Derby.

ABOVE: Looking up Pine Mountain from Pineville, it seems that a huge rock outcropping is ready to roll right down the hill, so locals loved to tease visitors that only a huge chain kept the rock in place. In the 1930s, some Pineville Kiwanians and Civilian Conservation Corps members hauled this gigantic chain up the mountainside and attached it to "prove" the tall tale.

LEFT: Centerpiece of its namesake state resort park, Cumberland Falls drops sixty-eight feet. Mist from the rocks below makes it one of the few falls on Earth that produce "moonbows" on brightly moonlit nights.

FOLLOWING PAGE: A lone hackberry tree marks the end of day.